Assessment

Columbus, OH

SRAonline.com

 **SRA**

Copyright © 2005 by SRA/McGraw-Hill.

All rights reserved. Except as permitted under the United States Copyright Act, no part of this publication may be reproduced or distributed in any form or by any means, or stored in a database or retrieval system, without the prior written permission of the publisher, unless otherwise indicated.

Send all inquiries to:
SRA/McGraw-Hill
8787 Orion Place
Columbus, OH 43240-4027

Printed in the United States of America.

ISBN 0-07-601859-8

2 3 4 5 6 7 8 9 MAZ 10 09 08 07 06 05 04

The **McGraw·Hill** Companies

Table of Contents

Assessment in Art 5
Evaluation Checklists 6

Unit 1 Line

Lesson 1 Thick and Thin Lines 9
Lesson 2 Lines Can Make Calm Pictures 11
Lesson 3 Lines Can Make Busy Pictures 13
Lesson 4 Curved Lines 15
Lesson 5 Smooth and Rough Lines 17
Lesson 6 Broken Lines 19

Unit 2 Shape

Lesson 1 Shape 21
Lesson 2 Geometric Shapes 23
Lesson 3 Free-Form Shapes 25
Lesson 4 More About Shapes 27
Lesson 5 Body Shapes 29
Lesson 6 The Shape of People 31

Unit 3 Color

Lesson 1 A Garden of Colors 33
Lesson 2 Recognizing Objects by Color 35
Lesson 3 Looking at Colors 37
Lesson 4 Primary Colors 39
Lesson 5 Colors Show Feelings 41
Lesson 6 Light and Dark Colors 43

Unit 4 Space and Form

Lesson 1 Space in Art 45
Lesson 2 Form 47
Lesson 3 Space and Form 49
Lesson 4 A Building Is a Form 51
Lesson 5 An Animal Is a Form 53
Lesson 6 Forms Can Be Used 55

Level K

Unit 5 Texture

Lesson 1 Texture You Can Touch 57
Lesson 2 Texture You Can See 59
Lesson 3 Designing with Texture 61
Lesson 4 Fiber Textures 63
Lesson 5 Real Texture on Forms 65
Lesson 6 Texture on Shapes 67

Unit 6 Principles of Art

Lesson 1 Pattern 69
Lesson 2 Rhythm and Movement 71
Lesson 3 Balance 73
Lesson 4 Balance in Sculpture 75
Lesson 5 Unity 77
Lesson 6 Unity in Sculpture 79

Answer Key 81

Creative Expression Rubrics 87

Assessment in Art

"Assessment provides the basis for schools to be accountable to their communities for student learning in all subjects. As such, assessment is also an important part of a good art education. Assessment occurs during as well as after the art lesson. It provides some assurance that students are learning what teachers intend to teach."

—Carmen L. Armstrong
Designing Assessment in Art. National Art Education Association, 1994

Quality art programs require students to engage in problem solving, visual discrimination, and critical and creative thinking processes. These processes include visual memory, communication, comparing and contrasting, predicting, hypothesizing, and evaluating. Art education teaches key concepts and skills such as shape, color recognition, size differentiation, letter and number recognition, listening skills, sequencing, following directions, hand-eye and motor coordination, kinesthetic and spatial relationships, and direction and location. A valid assessment of an art program can demonstrate that students are, in fact, developing these essential skills.

There are a variety of *Art Connections* assessment tools available to art educators.

- **Blackline master assessments** in this book evaluate a student's understanding of the elements and principles of art presented in each lesson of the *Art Connections* program. There are 36 English and Spanish blackline master assessments, one for each lesson. These assessments can be used individually, following each lesson, or they can be grouped and used two or three times during a unit.

- **Evaluation Checklists** for Art History and Culture, Art Criticism, Aesthetic Perception, Creative Expression, and Portfolio Assessment presented on the following pages are intended to be flexible so that teachers can adjust them to various classroom and individual needs. These checklists can be used at the teacher's discretion. They are intended to be copied for each evaluation and may be kept in each student's art portfolio. Each accomplishment on the Evaluation Checklists is designed to be rated on a three-point scale.

    3—Established. The student's response or work demonstrates understanding and competence.
    2—Emerging. The student demonstrates some degree of knowledge and skill.
    1—Not yet. There is not yet evidence in the student's work that he or she has grasped the skill.

- **Creative Expression** rubrics provide valuable guidance for assessing the artwork that students create in class. There are 36 Creative Expression rubrics, one for each lesson in the *Art Connections* program.

Name _____ Date _____ Lesson _____

Evaluation Checklists

Art History and Culture

Accomplishment	Not Applicable	Not Yet 1	Emerging 2	Established 3	Notes
Compares and contrasts artwork by different artists					
Recognizes artist's culture					
Recognizes artist's style					
Identifies artwork's place of origin					
Identifies artist's work					
Identifies subject matter of artwork					
Identifies cultural symbols in artwork					
Understands that art is practiced by all cultures, past and present					
Identifies time period of artwork					
Uses appropriate art vocabulary in describing, interpreting, or reflecting on artwork					

Art Criticism

Accomplishment	Not Applicable	Not Yet 1	Emerging 2	Established 3	Notes
Describes the elements and principles of art used in a work					
Analyzes artwork effectively					
Interprets the meaning and purpose of artwork					
Judges artwork according to specific criteria					
Uses appropriate art vocabulary in describing, interpreting, or reflecting on artwork					
Identifies a variety of art career opportunities					
Recognizes artist's purpose or main idea of the work					
Supports analysis, interpretation, and judgments with examples					

Evaluation Checklist   Level K

Name _____ Date _____ Lesson _____

Evaluation Checklists

Aesthetic Perception

Accomplishment	Not Applicable	Not Yet 1	Emerging 2	Established 3	Notes
Describes the multisensory characteristics in a work of art					
Uses appropriate art vocabulary in describing, interpreting, or reflecting on artwork					
Recognizes connections between art and other disciplines					
Compares and contrasts visual characteristics of objects and subjects					
Recognizes similarities and differences between visual art and music, dance, and theatre					
Demonstrates ability to observe elements and principles of art in the environment					
Draws appropriate conclusions based on aesthetic perception					

Creative Expression

Accomplishment	Not Applicable	Not Yet 1	Emerging 2	Established 3	Notes
Knows the differences between materials, techniques, and processes					
Uses different media, techniques, and processes to communicate ideas, experiences, and stories					
Uses art materials and tools in a safe and responsible manner					
Understands and effectively uses the elements and principles of art to communicate ideas					
Creates original, imaginative, and inventive works of art in 2-D and 3-D					
Demonstrates skill and craftsmanship					

Level K   Evaluation Checklist   **7**

Name _____ Date _____ Lesson _____

Evaluation Checklists

Portfolio Assessment

Accomplishment	Not Applicable	Not Yet 1	Emerging 2	Established 3	Notes
Completeness: Artwork in portfolio meets assigned requirements					
Effort: Artwork demonstrates concerted effort					
Variety: Artwork in portfolio demonstrates a variety of media, techniques, and processes					
Skill: Artwork demonstrates ability to utilize elements and principles of art to communicate ideas					
Volume: Portfolio includes a sufficient amount of work					
Quality: Artwork demonstrates appropriate level of quality					
Risk-Taking: Artwork demonstrates taking risks in creating/choosing works that go beyond minimum expectations					
Growth: Artwork demonstrates improvement					
Self-Evaluation: Student shows awareness of strengths and weaknesses					

Name _____ Date _____ Lesson **1** UNIT 1

Thick and Thin Lines

1	2
3	4

For the teacher: Use the following prompts for this activity.
1. Using a crayon, draw a thin line in box 1.
2. Draw a thick line in box 2.
3. Draw thick and thin lines in box 3.
4. Draw something you see in the room that has thick or thin lines in box 4.

Level K   Unit 1 • An Introduction to Line   **9**

Nombre _____ Fecha _____

Lección 1
UNIDAD 1

Líneas gruesas y líneas finas

1	2
3	4

Para el maestro: Usa las siguientes instrucciones para esta actividad.
1. Con un creyón, dibujen una línea fina en la caja 1.
2. Dibujen una línea gruesa en la caja 2.
3. Dibujen líneas gruesas y finas en la caja 3.
4. Dibujen en la caja 4 algo que vean en el cuarto que tiene líneas gruesas o finas.

10 Unidad 1 • Una introducción a la línea   Nivel K

Name _____ Date _____

Lines Can Make Calm Pictures

Lesson **2** UNIT 1

1	2
3	4

For the teacher: Use the following prompts for this activity.
1. Using a crayon, draw a vertical line in box 1.
2. Draw a horizontal line in box 2.
3. Draw something you see in the room that has a vertical line in box 3.
4. Draw a picture using both vertical and horizontal lines in box 4.

Level K　　　　　　　　　　　　　　　Unit 1 • An Introduction to Line　**11**

Nombre _____ Fecha _____

Lección 2
UNIDAD 1

Las líneas pueden formar dibujos tranquilos

1	2
3	4

Para el maestro: Usa las siguientes instrucciones para esta actividad.
1. Con un creyón, dibujen una línea vertical en la caja 1.
2. Dibujen una línea horizontal en la caja 2.
3. Dibujen en la caja 3 algo que vean en el cuarto que tiene una línea vertical.
4. Dibujen un cuadro usando líneas verticales y horizontales en la caja 4.

Unidad 1 • Una introducción a la línea

Nivel K

Name _____ Date _____ Lesson **3** UNIT 1

Lines Can Make Busy Pictures

1	2
3	4

For the teacher: Use the following prompts for this activity.
1. Using a crayon, draw a diagonal line in box 1.
2. Draw a zigzag line in box 2.
3. Draw something you see in the room that has a diagonal line in box 3.
4. Draw a picture using both diagonal and zigzag lines in box 4.

Level K   Unit 1 • An Introduction to Line   **13**

Nombre _____ Fecha _____

Lección 3 UNIDAD 1

Las líneas pueden hacer cuadros ocupados

1	2
3	4

Para el maestro: Usa las siguientes instrucciones para esta actividad.
1. Con un creyón, dibujen una línea diagonal en la caja 1.
2. Dibujen una línea en zigzag en la caja 2.
3. Dibujen en la caja 3 algo que vean en el cuarto que tiene una línea diagonal.
4. Dibujen un cuadro usando líneas diagonales y en zigzag en la caja 4.

14 Unidad 1 • Una introducción a la línea

Nivel K

Name _____ Date _____ Lesson **4** UNIT 1

Curved Lines

1	2
3	4

For the teacher: Use the following prompts for this activity.
1. Using a crayon, draw a curvy line in box 1.
2. Draw a vertical line in box 2.
3. Draw something that appears to be moving in box 3.
4. Draw something that appears to be still in box 4.

Level K   Unit 1 • An Introduction to Line   **15**

Nombre _____ Fecha _____

Lección 4
UNIDAD 1

Líneas curvadas

1	2
3	4

Para el maestro: Usa las siguientes instrucciones para esta actividad.
1. Con un creyón, dibujen una línea curva en la caja 1.
2. Dibujen una línea vertical en la caja 2.
3. Dibujen algo que parezca moverse en la caja 3.
4. Dibujen algo que parezca inmóvil en la caja 4.

Unidad 1 • Una introducción a la línea

Nivel K

Name _____ Date _____ Lesson **5** UNIT 1

Smooth and Rough Lines

1	2
3	4

For the teacher: Use the following prompts for this activity.
1. Using a crayon or pencil, draw a smooth line in box 1.
2. Draw a rough line in box 2.
3. Draw a picture of something that looks smooth in box 3.
4. Draw a picture of something that looks rough in box 4.

Level K   Unit 1 • An Introduction to Line   **17**

Nombre _____ Fecha _____

Lección 5
UNIDAD 1

Líneas suaves y ásperas

1	2
3	4

Para el maestro: Usa las siguientes instrucciones para esta actividad.
1. Con un creyón o lápiz, dibujen una línea suave en la caja 1.
2. Dibujen una línea áspera en la caja 2.
3. Dibujen un cuadro de algo que parezca suave en la caja 3.
4. Dibujen un cuadro de algo que parezca áspero en la caja 4.

18   Unidad 1 • Una introducción a la línea   Nivel K

Name _____ Date _____ Lesson **6** UNIT 1

Broken Lines

For the teacher: Use the following prompts for this activity.
1. Using a crayon or pencil, draw a solid line in box 1.
2. Draw a broken line in box 2.

Level K   Unit 1 • An Introduction to Line   19

Nombre _____ Fecha _____

Lección 6 UNIDAD 1

Líneas entrecortadas

Para el maestro: Usa las siguientes instrucciones para esta actividad.
1. Con un creyón o lápiz, dibujen una línea continua en la caja 1.
2. Dibujen una línea entrecortada en la caja 2.

Name _____ Date _____

Lesson **1**
UNIT 2

Shape

1	2
3	4

For the teacher: Use the following prompt for this activity.
Look for shapes in the artwork by Mercer Mayer. Using a crayon, draw some of the shapes you find. Draw a different shape in each of the boxes.

Level K Unit 2 • An Introduction to Shape **21**

Nombre _____ Fecha _____

Lección 1 UNIDAD 2

La figura

1	2
3	4

Para el maestro: Usa la siguiente instrucción para esta actividad.
Busquen figuras en la obra de arte de Mercer Mayer. Con un creyón, dibujen algunas de las figuras que consigan. Dibujen una figura diferente en cada uno de las cajas.

Unidad 2 • Una introducción a la forma

Nivel K

Name _____ Date _____ Lesson 2 UNIT 2

Geometric Shapes

1	2
3	4

For the teacher: Use the following prompts for this activity.
1. Use a crayon to draw a square in box 1.
2. Draw a circle in box 2.
3. Draw a triangle in box 3.
4. Draw a rectangle in box 4.

Level K   Unit 2 • An Introduction to Shape

Nombre _____ Fecha _____

Lección 2
UNIDAD 2

Las figuras geométricas

1	2
3	4

Para el maestro: Usa las siguientes instrucciones para esta actividad.
1. Con un creyón, dibujen un cuadrado en la caja 1.
2. Dibujen un círculo en la caja 2.
3. Dibujen un triángulo en la caja 3.
4. Dibujen un rectángulo en la caja 4.

Unidad 2 • Una introducción a la forma

Nivel K

Name _____ Date _____ Lesson **3** UNIT 2

Free-Form Shapes

For the teacher: Use the following prompts for this activity.
1. Use a crayon or a pencil to draw an imaginary free-form shape in box 1.
2. Draw something you know and can see that is a free-form shape in box 2.

Nombre _____ Fecha _____

Lección 3
UNIDAD 2

Las figuras abstractas

Para el maestro: Usa las siguientes instrucciones para esta actividad.
1. Con un creyón o un lápiz, dibujen una figura abstracta en la caja 1.
2. En la caja 2, dibujen algo que sepan y que puedan ver que es una figura abstracta.

Unidad 2 • Una introducción a la forma

Nivel K

Name _____ Date _____ Lesson 4 UNIT 2

More About Shapes

For the teacher: Use the following prompts for this activity.
1. Use a crayon or a pencil to draw a free-form shape in box 1.
2. Draw a geometric shape in box 2.

Level K   Unit 2 • An Introduction to Shape   27

Nombre _____ Fecha _____

Lección 4
UNIDAD 2

Más acerca de las figuras

Para el maestro: Usa las siguientes instrucciones para esta actividad.
1. Con un creyón o un lápiz, dibujen una figura abstracta en la caja 1.
2. Dibujen una figura geométrica en la caja 2.

Unidad 2 • Una introducción a la forma

Nivel K

Name _____ Date _____ Lesson **5** UNIT 2

Body Shapes

For the teacher: Use the following prompts for this activity.
1. Use a crayon or a pencil to trace your hand with your fingers together in box 1.
2. Draw the shape of your hand without tracing it in box 2. The shapes should be similar.

Level K　　　　　　　　　　　　Unit 2 • An Introduction to Shape　　**29**

Nombre _____ Fecha _____ Lección **5** UNIDAD 2

Las figuras corporales

Para el maestro: Usa las siguientes instrucciones para esta actividad.
1. Con un creyón o un lápiz, tracen su mano con los dedos juntos en la caja 1.
2. Dibujen la figura de su mano sin trazarla en la caja 2. Las figuras deben ser parecidas.

Unidad 2 • Una introducción a la forma   Nivel K

Name _____ Date _____ Lesson **6** UNIT 2

The Shape of People

For the teacher: Use the following prompt for this activity.
Use a crayon to draw a series of five different geometric shapes from small to large in the box.

Level K   Unit 2 • An Introduction to Shape   31

Nombre _____ Fecha _____

Lección **6** UNIDAD 2

La figura de las personas

Para el maestro: Usa la siguiente instrucción para esta actividad.
Con un creyón, dibujen en la caja una serie de cinco figuras geométricas diferentes desde la más pequeña hasta la más grande.

32 Unidad 2 • Una introducción a la forma

Nivel K

Name _____ Date _____ Lesson 1 UNIT 3

A Garden of Colors

For the teacher: Use the following prompts for this activity.
1. Using a crayon, color a different color in each box.
2. Say the name of each color out loud.

Nombre _____ Fecha _____

Lección **1**
UNIDAD 3

Un jardín de colores

Para el maestro: Usa las siguientes instrucciones para esta actividad.
1. Con un creyón, coloreen cada cuadro con un color diferente.
2. Digan en voz alta el nombre de cada color.

Unidad 3 • El color

Nivel K

Name _____ Date _____ Lesson 2 UNIT 3

Recognizing Objects by Color

| 1 | 2 |

For the teacher: Use the following prompt for this activity.
Using a crayon, draw an object in each box that is identified by its color.

Level K Unit 3 • Color 35

Nombre _____ Fecha _____

Lección 2
UNIDAD 3

Reconocer los objetos por el color

1	2

Para el maestro: Usa la siguiente instrucción para esta actividad.
Con un creyón, dibujen un objeto en cada cuadro que se identifique por su color.

Unidad 3 • El color

Nivel K

Name _____ Date _____ Lesson **3** UNIT 3

Looking at Colors

1	2
3	4

For the teacher: Use the following prompt for this activity.
Using only one crayon, draw a different object of that color in each box.

Level K   Unit 3 • Color   **37**

Nombre _____ Fecha _____

Lección **3**
UNIDAD 3

Mirar los colores

1	2
3	4

Para el maestro: Usa la siguiente instrucción para esta actividad.
Con un solo creyón, dibujen un objeto diferente de ese color en cada cuadro.

Unidad 3 • El color

Nivel K

Name _____ Date _____ Lesson **4** UNIT 3

Primary Colors

For the teacher: Use the following prompt for this activity.
Using crayons, draw a picture using only the primary colors.

Level K   Unit 3 • Color   **39**

Nombre _____ Fecha _____

Lección 4
UNIDAD 3

Los colores primarios

Para el maestro: Usa la siguiente instrucción para esta actividad.
Usando creyones, hagan un dibujo usando sólo los colores primarios.

40 Unidad 3 • El color Nivel K

Name _____ Date _____ Lesson 5 UNIT 3

Colors Show Feelings

1	2
3	4

For the teacher: Use the following prompts for this activity.
1. Using a crayon, draw a line using a color that represents a happy feeling in box 1.
2. Draw a line using a color that represents a sad feeling in box 2.
3. Draw a line using a color that represents an angry feeling in box 3.
4. Draw a line using a color that represents a silly feeling in box 4.

Level K   Unit 3 • Color

Nombre _____ Fecha _____

Lección 5
UNIDAD 3

Los colores muestran sentimientos

1	2
3	4

Para el maestro: Usa las siguientes instrucciones para esta actividad.
1. Con un creyón, tracen una línea usando un color que represente un sentimiento feliz en el cuadro 1.
2. Tracen una línea usando un color que represente un sentimiento triste en el cuadro 2.
3. Tracen una línea usando un color que represente un sentimiento de enojo en el cuadro 3.
4. Tracen una línea usando un color que represente un sentimiento tonto en el cuadro 4.

42   Unidad 3 • El color   Nivel K

Name _____ Date _____ Lesson **6** UNIT 3

Light and Dark Colors

For the teacher: Use the following prompts for this activity.
1. Find four different pictures of the same color in a magazine.
2. Sort the pictures according to value and glue them in the box in order from lightest to darkest.

Level K   Unit 3 • Color   **43**

Nombre _____ Fecha _____

Lección 6
UNIDAD 3

Los colores claros y oscuros

Para el maestro: Usa las siguientes instrucciones para esta actividad.
1. En una revista, busquen cuatro dibujos diferentes del mismo color.
2. Clasifiquen los dibujos según el valor y péguenlos en el cuadro en orden del más claro al más oscuro.

Unidad 3 • El color   Nivel K

Name _____ Date _____ Lesson 1 UNIT 4

Space in Art

For the teacher: Use the following prompts for this activity.
1. Using a blue crayon, draw a shape in the center of the box.
2. Color the space around the shape with a red crayon.

Level K Unit 4 • Space and Form **45**

Nombre _____ Fecha _____

Lección 1 · UNIDAD 4

El espacio en el arte

Para el maestro: Usa las siguientes instrucciones para esta actividad.
1. Con un creyón azul, dibujen una figura en el centro del cuadro.
2. Coloreen el espacio alrededor de la figura con un creyón rojo.

Name _____ Date _____ Lesson **2** UNIT 4

Form

1

2

For the teacher: Use the following prompts for this activity.
1. Using a crayon, draw a large circle in each box.
2. In box 2, add color, stripes, and lines to the circle to make it look like a three-dimensional form that can be seen from all sides.

Level K   Unit 4 • Space and Form   47

Nombre _____ Fecha _____

Lección 2
UNIDAD 4

La forma

1

2

Para el maestro: Usa las siguientes instrucciones para esta actividad.
1. Con un creyón, dibujen un círculo grande en cada cuadro.
2. En cuadro 2, agreguen color, rayas y líneas al círculo para que parezca como una forma tridimensional que se puede ver desde todos los lados.

48 Unidad 4 • El espacio y la forma

Nivel K

Name _____ Date _____ Lesson 3 UNIT 4

Space and Form

For the teacher: Use the following prompts for this activity.
1. Using a crayon, draw a large circle.
2. Add color, stripes, and lines to the circle to make it look like a three-dimensional form that can be seen from all sides.
3. Color the space around the circle with a green crayon.

Level K   Unit 4 • Space and Form

Nombre _____ Fecha _____

Lección 3
UNIDAD 4

La figura y la forma

Para el maestro: Usa las siguientes instrucciones para esta actividad.
1. Con un creyón, dibujen un círculo grande.
2. Agreguen color, rayas y líneas al círculo para que parezca una forma tridimensional que se puede ver desde todos los lados.
3. Coloreen el espacio alrededor del círculo con un creyón verde.

Unidad 4 • El espacio y la forma

Nivel K

Name _____ Date _____ Lesson 4 UNIT 4

A Building Is a Form

For the teacher: Use the following prompts for this activity.
Using geometric shapes, draw the parts of a building. First, draw the bottom.
Then, add shapes onto the sides. Next, add shapes to make a roof.

Level K   Unit 4 • Space and Form   51

Nombre _____ Fecha _____

Lección 4
UNIDAD 4

Un edificio es una forma

Para el maestro: Usa las siguientes instrucciones para esta actividad.
Usando figuras geométricas, dibujen las partes de un edificio. Primero, dibujen la parte de abajo. Luego, agreguen figuras a los lados. Después, agreguen figuras para hacer el techo.

Unidad 4 • El espacio y la forma

Nivel K

Name _____ Date _____

Lesson 5 UNIT 4

An Animal Is a Form

For the teacher: Use the following prompts for this activity.
Make an animal. Draw a large circle for the body and a smaller circle for the head. Then, use other shapes for the ears, legs, and tail.

Level K   Unit 4 • Space and Form   53

Nombre _____ Fecha _____

Lección 5
UNIDAD 4

Un animal es una forma

Para el maestro: Usa las siguientes instrucciones para esta actividad.
Hagan un animal. Dibujen un círculo grande para el cuerpo y un círculo pequeño para la cabeza. Luego, usen otras figuras para las orejas, las patas y la cola.

Name _____ Date _____

Lesson **6** UNIT 4

Forms Can Be Used

1	2
3	4

For the teacher: Use the following prompt for this activity.
In each box, use a crayon to draw one of the pots created by your classmates.

Level K Unit 4 • Space and Form

Nombre _____ Fecha _____

Lección 6
UNIDAD 4

Las formas se pueden usar

1	2
3	4

Para el maestro: Usa la siguiente instrucción para esta actividad.
En cada cuadro, usen un creyón para dibujar uno de los envases creados por sus compañeros.

56   Unidad 4 • El espacio y la forma   Nivel K

Name _____ Date _____ Lesson 1 UNIT 5

Texture You Can Touch

1

2

For the teacher: Use the following prompts for this activity.
1. In box 1, use crayons to draw a picture of something that feels smooth.
2. In box 2, draw a picture of something that feels rough.

Level K   Unit 5 • Texture   **57**

Nombre _____ Fecha _____

Lección 1
UNIDAD 5

La textura que puedes tocar

1

2

Para el maestro: Usa las siguientes instrucciones para esta actividad.
1. En el cuadro 1, usen creyones para hacer un dibujo de algo que se sienta suave.
2. En el cuadro 2, hagan un dibujo de algo que se sienta áspero.

Name _____ Date _____ **Lesson 2** UNIT 5

Texture You Can See

1	2

For the teacher: Use the following prompts for this activity.
1. In box 1, use crayons to draw the lines or shapes that create a rough visual texture.
2. In box 2, draw lines that create a smooth visual texture.

Level K   Unit 5 • Texture   **59**

Nombre _____ Fecha _____

Lección **2** UNIDAD 5

La textura que puedes ver

1	2

Para el maestro: Usa las siguientes instrucciones para esta actividad.
1. En el primer cuadro, usen creyones para trazar las líneas o figuras que crean una textura visual áspera.
2. En el segundo cuadro, tracen líneas que crean una textura visual suave.

Name _____ Date _____ Lesson **3** UNIT 5

Designing with Texture

For the teacher: Use the following prompt for this activity.
Using crayons, draw a puppet. Show different textures by drawing yarn hair, furry jackets, or silky shirts.

Level K   Unit 5 • Texture   **61**

Nombre _____ Fecha _____

Lección 3
UNIDAD 5

Diseñar con textura

Para el maestro: Usa las siguientes instrucciones para esta actividad.
Con creyones, dibujen un títere. Muestren diferentes texturas al dibujar pelo de estambre, chaquetas peludas o camisas de seda.

Name _____ Date _____ Lesson 4 UNIT 5

Fiber Textures

For the teacher: Use the following prompt for this activity.
Using crayons, draw a picture of baskets. Show straw, yarn, cloth, canvas, or wooden baskets.

Level K Unit 5 • Texture

Nombre _____ Fecha _____

Lección 4
UNIDAD 5

Las texturas fibrosas

Para el maestro: Usa la siguiente instrucción para esta actividad. Con creyones, hagan un dibujo de cestas. Muestren cestas de paja, estambre o hilo, lona o madera.

Unidad 5 • La textura

Nivel K

Name _____ Date _____ Lesson **5** UNIT 5

Real Texture on Forms

1

2

For the teacher: Use the following prompts for this activity.
1. In box 1, use crayons to draw the lines and shapes you used on your clay to show smooth texture.
2. In box 2, draw the lines and shapes you used to show rough texture.

Level K   Unit 5 • Texture   **65**

Nombre _____ Fecha _____

Lección 5 UNIDAD 5

La textura real en las formas

1

2

Para el maestro: Usa las siguientes instrucciones para esta actividad.
1. En el primer cuadro, usen creyones para dibujar las líneas y figuras que usaron con su plastilina para mostrar la textura suave.
2. En el segundo cuadro, dibujen las líneas y figuras que usaron para mostrar la textura áspera.

66 Unidad 5 • La textura

Nivel K

Name _____ Date _____ Lesson **6** UNIT 5

Texture on Shapes

For the teacher: Use the following prompt for this activity.
Using crayons, draw pictures of two things with different kinds of stitching.

Level K   Unit 5 • Texture   **67**

Nombre _____ Fecha _____

Lección 6
UNIDAD 5

La textura en las figuras

Para el maestro: Usa la siguiente instrucción para esta actividad. Con creyones, dibujen dos cosas con diferentes tipos de puntada.

68 Unidad 5 • La textura

Nivel K

Name _____ Date _____ Lesson 2 UNIT 6

Rhythm and Movement

1	2

For the teacher: Use the following prompts for this activity.
1. Using crayons, draw circles in box 1 that show quick movement.
2. Draw circles in box 2 that show slow movement.

Level K   Unit 6 • Principals of Art   71

Nombre _____ Fecha _____

Lección 2
UNIDAD 6

El ritmo y el movimiento

| 1 | 2 |

Para el maestro: Usa las siguientes instrucciones para esta actividad.
1. Con creyones, dibujen círculos en el cuadro 1 que muestren un movimiento rápido.
2. Dibujen círculos en el cuadro 2 que muestren un movimiento lento.

72 Unidad 6 • Los principales del arte

Nivel K

Name _____ Date _____ Lesson **3** UNIT 6

Balance

| 1 | 2 |

For the teacher: Use the following prompts for this activity.
1. Using crayons, draw a shape in box 1.
2. Draw the same shape in box 2 to create balance.
3. Repeat this activity with a different set of shapes.

Level K   Unit 6 • Principals of Art

Nombre _____ Fecha _____

Lección **3**
UNIDAD 6

El equilibrio

1	2

Para el maestro: Usa las siguientes instrucciones para esta actividad.
1. Con creyones, dibujen una figura en el cuadro 1.
2. Dibujen la misma figura en el cuadro 2 para crear equilibrio.
3. Repitan esta actividad con diferentes grupos de figuras.

Unidad 6 • Los principales del arte

Nivel K

Name _____ Date _____ Lesson 4 UNIT 6

Balance in Sculpture

For the teacher: Use the following prompt for this activity.
Using crayons, draw a creature that has balance.

Level K   Unit 6 • Principals of Art   75

Nombre _____ Fecha _____

Lección **4** UNIDAD 6

El equilibrio en la escultura

Para el maestro: Usa la siguiente instrucción para esta actividad.
Con creyones, dibujen una criatura que tenga equilibrio.

76 Unidad 6 • Los principales del arte

Nivel K

Name _____ Date _____ Lesson **5** UNIT 6

Unity

For the teacher: Use the following prompt for this activity.
Using crayons, create a drawing that has unity. Show a group of people who are enjoying an activity together.

Level K Unit 6 • Principals of Art **77**

Nombre _____ Fecha _____

Lección 5
UNIDAD 6

La unidad

Para el maestro: Usa la siguiente instrucción para esta actividad.
Con creyones, hagan un dibujo que tenga unidad. Muestren un grupo de personas que están disfrutando juntos de una actividad.

78 Unidad 6 • Los principales del arte

Nivel K

Name _____ Date _____ Lesson **6** UNIT 6

Unity in Sculpture

For the teacher: Use the following prompt for this activity.
Using crayons, create a drawing that has unity. Show of a set of animals in your drawing.

Level K   Unit 6 • Principals of Art   **79**

Nombre _____ Fecha _____

Lección
6
UNIDAD 6

La unidad en la escultura

Para el maestro: Usa la siguiente instrucción para esta actividad.
Con creyones, hagan un dibujo que tenga unidad. Muestren un grupo de animales en su dibujo.

Answer Key

Unit 1

Lesson 1
Students should draw a thin line in box 1, a thick line in box 2, and thick and thin lines in box 3. Drawings will vary in box 4.

Lesson 2
Students should draw a vertical line in box 1 and a horizontal line in box 2. Answers will vary in box 3 but should have a vertical line. Drawings will vary in box 4 but should have both vertical and horizontal lines.

Lesson 3
Students should draw a diagonal line in box 1 and a zigzag line in box 2. Answers will vary in box 3 but should have a diagonal line. Drawings will vary in box 4 but should have both diagonal and zigzag lines.

Lesson 4
Students should draw a curved line in box 1 and a vertical line in box 2. Students should use curved lines to draw something that appears to be moving in box 3 and vertical or horizontal lines to draw something that appears to be still in box 4.

Lesson 5
Students should draw a smooth line in box 1 and a rough line in box 2. Drawings will vary in box 3 but the object should look smooth. Drawings will vary in box 4 but the object should look rough.

Lesson 6
Students should draw a solid line in box 1 and a broken line in box 2.

Answer Key

Unit 2

Lesson 1
Drawings will vary, but each box should show a different shape.

Lesson 2
Students should draw a square in box 1, a circle in box 2, a triangle in box 3, and a rectangle in box 4.

Lesson 3
Answers will vary in box 1 but should represent an imaginary free-form shape. Drawings will vary in box 2 but should be a recognizable free-form shape.

Lesson 4
Students should draw a free-form shape in box 1 and a geometric shape in box 2.

Lesson 5
Students should trace a hand in box 1. In box 2, they will draw the same hand without tracing.

Lesson 6
Drawings will vary but should include five different geometric shapes in order from smallest to largest.

Answer Key

Unit 3

Lesson 1
Colors will vary. Students should color space in each box a different color and name the colors.

Lesson 2
Drawings will vary. In each box the students will draw an object that is identified by its color; for example, an orange, a blueberry, or a purple grape.

Lesson 3
Drawings will vary. Students will use one color to draw four different objects of the same color.

Lesson 4
Drawings will vary, but students should use only red, yellow, and blue crayons.

Lesson 5
Drawings will vary. In box 1, students should draw a line using a color that represents happiness; in box 2, sadness; in box 3, anger, and box 4, silliness.

Lesson 6
Students will cut out magazine pictures of objects that are the same color and arrange them on the page in order from lightest to darkest.

Answer Key

Unit 4

Lesson 1
Drawings will vary, but a blue geometric or free-form shape should be drawn in the center of the page with red filling the space around the shape.

Lesson 2
The circle in box 1 should be only an outline of a circle. The circle in box 2 should have areas filled in with color(s), stripes, and lines.

Lesson 3
Students should draw a circle that has color(s), stripes, and lines to make it look like a three-dimensional form. The space around the circle should be colored green.

Lesson 4
Drawings will vary. Students should use geometric shapes, such as a rectangle for the base, a triangle for the roof, squares for windows, and another rectangle for the door, when drawing their building.

Lesson 5
Drawings will vary, but students should include a circle for the main body, another circle for the head, and possibly triangles for ears, rectangles for legs, squares for feet, and another shape for the tail.

Lesson 6
Shapes will vary but might include geometric shapes and/or free-form shapes. Check to see that students have drawn four different shapes, one in each box.

Answer Key

Unit 5

Lesson 1
Drawings in box 1 will vary but might include a glass, a plate, or any other smooth-surfaced item. Drawings in box 2 will vary but might include a pinecone, a rock, or any rough-surfaced item.

Lesson 2
Drawings will vary in box 1 but could include lines that are zigzags, sharp-cornered shapes, or shapes that have a pattern on them. Drawings in box 2 could include curvy lines, straight lines, or rounded shapes.

Lesson 3
Drawings will vary but could include clothing that has different patterns of lines and shapes.

Lesson 4
Drawings will vary but could include baskets with different patterns on the sides, such as zigzag or curvy lines or geometric patterns.

Lesson 5
Drawings in box 1 will vary but could include smooth, straight, or curvy lines, or rounded shapes. In box 2, drawings will vary but might include lines that zigzag and shapes with sharp corners.

Lesson 6
Drawings will vary but should include four different patterns or shapes. These might include cross-stitches, dotted lines, or curly lines.

Level K

Answer Key

Unit 6

Lesson 1
Students should draw a repeating pattern of two or three shapes.

Lesson 2
Drawings will vary. Circles that show quick movement might be smaller and closer together than circles that show slow movement. It is possible that quick circles will also be misshapen.

Lesson 3
Students draw the same two shapes in both boxes.

Lesson 4
Drawings will vary. Students will draw a creature that has the same features on both sides so it has balance.

Lesson 5
Drawings will vary. Students should show a group of people participating in an activity together, such as dancing, eating dinner, or playing a game.

Lesson 6
Drawings will vary but should include a set of animals that belong together.

Name _____ Date _____ Lesson _____

Creative Expression Rubrics

Level K • Unit 1 • Lesson 1

	Art History and Culture	Aesthetic Perception	Creative Expression	Art Criticism
3 POINTS	The student demonstrates understanding that Native American culture is famous for its weaving tradition.	The student accurately distinguishes between thick and thin lines.	The student's painting clearly illustrates thick and thin lines.	The student thoughtfully and honestly evaluates his or her own work using the four steps of art criticism.
2 POINTS	The student's understanding that Native American culture is famous for its weaving tradition is weak or incomplete.	The student shows emerging awareness of thick and thin lines but cannot consistently identify them.	The student's painting shows some awareness of thick and thin lines.	The student attempts to evaluate his or her own work but shows an incomplete understanding of evaluation criteria.
1 POINT	The student cannot demonstrate understanding that Native American culture is famous for its weaving tradition.	The student cannot identify thick and thin lines.	The student's painting shows no understanding of thick and thin lines.	The student makes no attempt to evaluate his or her own artwork.

Level K • Unit 1 • Lesson 2

	Art History and Culture	Aesthetic Perception	Creative Expression	Art Criticism
3 POINTS	The student demonstrates understanding that artists from different times and places can use calm lines in their paintings.	The student accurately identifies vertical and horizontal lines in nature and fine art.	The student's landscape clearly illustrates vertical and horizontal lines.	The student thoughtfully and honestly evaluates his or her own work using the four steps of art criticism.
2 POINTS	The student's understanding that artists from different times and places can use calm lines in their paintings is weak or incomplete.	The student shows emerging awareness of vertical and horizontal lines but cannot consistently identify them.	The student's landscape shows some awareness of vertical and horizontal lines.	The student attempts to evaluate his or her own work but shows an incomplete understanding of evaluation criteria.
1 POINT	The student does not demonstrate understanding that artists from different times and places can use calm lines in their paintings.	The student cannot identify vertical or horizontal lines in nature or fine art.	The student's landscape shows no understanding of vertical and horizontal lines.	The student makes no attempt to evaluate his or her own artwork.

Level K — Creative Expression Rubrics

Name _____ Date _____ Lesson _____

Creative Expression Rubrics

Level K • Unit I • Lesson 3

	Art History and Culture	Aesthetic Perception	Creative Expression	Art Criticism
3 POINTS	The student recognizes that artists from different places use diagonal and zigzag lines to make exciting works of art.	The student accurately identifies and physically mimics diagonal and zigzag lines in his or her environment.	The student's drawing clearly illustrates diagonal and zigzag lines.	The student thoughtfully and honestly evaluates his or her own work using the four steps of art criticism.
2 POINTS	The student's recognition that artists from different places use diagonal and zigzag lines to make exciting works of art is weak or incomplete.	The student shows emerging awareness of diagonal and zigzag lines but cannot consistently identify them.	The student's drawing shows some awareness of diagonal and zigzag lines.	The student attempts to evaluate his or her own work but shows an incomplete understanding of evaluation criteria.
1 POINT	The student does not recognize that artists from different places use diagonal and zigzag lines to make exciting works of art.	The student cannot identify diagonal and zigzag lines.	The student's drawing shows no understanding of diagonal and zigzag lines.	The student makes no attempt to evaluate his or her own artwork.

Level K • Unit I • Lesson 4

	Art History and Culture	Aesthetic Perception	Creative Expression	Art Criticism
3 POINTS	The student recognizes that *The Fly* illustrates the story in the poem.	The student accurately describes the lines that arms, legs, and bodies make as they move.	The student's drawing clearly illustrates lines that show movement.	The student thoughtfully and honestly evaluates his or her own work using the four steps of art criticism.
2 POINTS	The student's recognition of *The Fly* as a story illustration is weak or incomplete.	The student shows emerging awareness of lines that show movement, but cannot consistently identify them.	The student's drawing shows some awareness of lines that show movement.	The student attempts to evaluate his or her own work but shows an incomplete understanding of evaluation criteria.
1 POINT	The student does not recognize that *The Fly* illustrates the story in the poem.	The student cannot identify lines that show movement.	The student's drawing shows no understanding of lines that show movement.	The student makes no attempt to evaluate his or her own artwork.

Name _____ Date _____ Lesson _____

Creative Expression Rubrics

Level K • Unit 1 • Lesson 5

	Art History and Culture	Aesthetic Perception	Creative Expression	Art Criticism
3 POINTS	The student recognizes that artists create works of art about different themes.	The student accurately locates smooth and rough lines in his or her artwork and the environment.	The student's drawing clearly illustrates smooth and rough lines.	The student thoughtfully and honestly evaluates his or her own work using the four steps of art criticism.
2 POINTS	The student's recognition that artists create works of art about different themes is weak or incomplete.	The student shows emerging awareness of smooth and rough lines but cannot consistently identify them.	The student's drawing shows some awareness of smooth and rough lines.	The student attempts to evaluate his or her own work but shows an incomplete understanding of evaluation criteria.
1 POINT	The student does not recognize that artists create works of art about different themes.	The student cannot identify smooth and rough lines.	The student's drawing shows no understanding of smooth and rough lines.	The student makes no attempt to evaluate his or her own artwork.

Level K • Unit 1 • Lesson 6

	Art History and Culture	Aesthetic Perception	Creative Expression	Art Criticism
3 POINTS	The student recognizes mosaics as a complex art form.	The student accurately locates broken lines in the environment.	The student's mosaic clearly illustrates broken lines.	The student thoughtfully and honestly evaluates his or her own work using the four steps of art criticism.
2 POINTS	The student's recognition of mosaics as a complex art form is weak or incomplete.	The student shows emerging awareness of broken lines but cannot consistently identify them.	The student's mosaic shows some awareness of broken lines.	The student attempts to evaluate his or her own work but shows an incomplete understanding of evaluation criteria.
1 POINT	The student does not recognize mosaics as a complex art form.	The student cannot identify broken lines.	The student's mosaic shows no understanding of broken lines.	The student makes no attempt to evaluate his or her own artwork.

Level K   Creative Expression Rubrics

Name _____ Date _____ Lesson _____

Creative Expression Rubrics

Level K • Unit 2 • Lesson 1

	Art History and Culture	Aesthetic Perception	Creative Expression	Art Criticism
3 POINTS	The student observes that artists use imagination and identifies such use in fine art.	The student accurately recognizes that lines outline shapes.	The student's drawing clearly illustrates lines that outline shapes.	The student thoughtfully and honestly evaluates his or her own work using the four steps of art criticism.
2 POINTS	The student observes that artists use imagination and can sometimes identify such use in fine art.	The student shows emerging awareness that lines outline shapes.	The student's drawing shows some awareness of lines that outline shapes.	The student attempts to evaluate his or her own work but shows an incomplete understanding of evaluation criteria.
1 POINT	The student does not understand that artists use imagination and cannot identify such use in fine art.	The student does not recognize that lines outline shapes.	The student's drawing shows no understanding of lines that outline shapes.	The student makes no attempt to evaluate his or her own artwork.

Level K • Unit 2 • Lesson 2

	Art History and Culture	Aesthetic Perception	Creative Expression	Art Criticism
3 POINTS	The student recognizes that artists use geometric shapes to create art and can identify these shapes in fine art.	The student accurately identifies geometric shapes by name and locates them in fine art.	The student's design clearly illustrates geometric shapes.	The student thoughtfully and honestly evaluates his or her own work using the four steps of art criticism.
2 POINTS	The student shows emerging awareness that artists use geometric shapes to create art and can identify some shapes in fine art.	The student shows emerging awareness of geometric shapes.	The student's design shows some awareness of geometric shapes.	The student attempts to evaluate his or her own work but shows an incomplete understanding of evaluation criteria.
1 POINT	The student cannot recognize that artists use geometric shapes to create art and cannot identify these shapes in fine art.	The student cannot identify geometric shapes by name or locate them in fine art.	The student's design shows no understanding of geometric shapes.	The student makes no attempt to evaluate his or her own artwork.

Name _____ Date _____ Lesson _____

Creative Expression Rubrics

Level K • Unit 2 • Lesson 3

	Art History and Culture	Aesthetic Perception	Creative Expression	Art Criticism
3 POINTS	The student recognizes that illustrators are artists.	The student accurately locates free-form shapes in artwork and in the environment.	The student's leaf prints clearly illustrate free-form shapes.	The student thoughtfully and honestly evaluates his or her own work using the four steps of art criticism.
2 POINTS	The student's recognition that illustrators are artists is weak or incomplete.	The student shows emerging awareness of free-form shapes.	The student's leaf prints show some awareness of free-form shapes.	The student attempts to evaluate his or her own work but shows an incomplete understanding of evaluation criteria.
1 POINT	The student does not recognize that illustrators are artists.	The student cannot locate free-form shapes in artwork or in the environment.	The student's leaf prints show no understanding of free-form shapes.	The student makes no attempt to evaluate his or her own artwork.

Level K • Unit 2 • Lesson 4

	Art History and Culture	Aesthetic Perception	Creative Expression	Art Criticism
3 POINTS	The student recognizes that artists use geometric and free-form shapes to create works of art and can identify these shapes in fine art.	The student accurately locates geometric and free-form shapes in artwork and in his or her environment.	The student's drawing clearly illustrates geometric and free-form shapes.	The student thoughtfully and honestly evaluates his or her own work using the four steps of art criticism.
2 POINTS	The student shows emerging awareness that artists use geometric and free-form shapes to create works of art and can identify some shapes in fine art.	The student shows emerging awareness of geometric and free-form shapes.	The student's drawing shows some awareness of geometric and free-form shapes.	The student attempts to evaluate his or her own work but shows an incomplete understanding of evaluation criteria.
1 POINT	The student cannot recognize that artists use geometric and free-form shapes to create works of art and cannot identify these shapes in fine art.	The student cannot locate geometric and free-form shapes in artwork or in his or her environment.	The student's drawing shows no understanding of geometric or free-form shapes.	The student makes no attempt to evaluate his or her own artwork.

Name _____ Date _____ Lesson _____

Creative Expression Rubrics

Level K • Unit 2 • Lesson 5

	Art History and Culture	Aesthetic Perception	Creative Expression	Art Criticism
3 POINTS	The student recognizes that artists help us learn about different people and places.	The student recognizes major body parts and notes differences in size among them.	The student's drawing clearly illustrates body shapes.	The student thoughtfully and honestly evaluates his or her own work using the four steps of art criticism.
2 POINTS	The student shows emerging awareness that artists help us learn about different people and places.	The student shows emerging awareness of major body parts and differences in size among them.	The student's drawing shows some awareness of body shapes.	The student attempts to evaluate his or her own work but shows an incomplete understanding of evaluation criteria.
1 POINT	The student cannot recognize that artists help us learn about different people and places.	The student does not recognize major body parts or note differences in size among them.	The student's drawing shows no understanding of body shapes.	The student makes no attempt to evaluate his or her own artwork.

Level K • Unit 2 • Lesson 6

	Art History and Culture	Aesthetic Perception	Creative Expression	Art Criticism
3 POINTS	The student recognizes that artists from the same period use different materials and styles to tell stories about families.	The student accurately compares sizes of body shapes in relation to sizes of people.	The student's family portrait clearly illustrates various sizes of body shapes.	The student thoughtfully and honestly evaluates his or her own work using the four steps of art criticism.
2 POINTS	The student shows emerging awareness that artists from the same period use different materials and styles to tell stories about families.	The student shows emerging awareness of sizes of body shapes in relation to sizes of people.	The student's family portrait shows some awareness of various sizes of body shapes.	The student attempts to evaluate his or her own work but shows an incomplete understanding of evaluation criteria.
1 POINT	The student does not recognize that artists from the same period use different materials and styles to tell stories about families.	The student does not accurately compare sizes of body shapes in relation to sizes of people.	The student's family portrait shows no understanding of various sizes of body shapes.	The student makes no attempt to evaluate his or her own artwork.

Name _____ Date _____ Lesson _____

Creative Expression Rubrics

Level K • Unit 3 • Lesson 1

	Art History and Culture	Aesthetic Perception	Creative Expression	Art Criticism
3 POINTS	The student recognizes that artists use different colors to create landscapes.	The student accurately locates colors in the artwork and in the environment.	The student's drawing clearly shows a variety of colors.	The student thoughtfully and honestly evaluates his or her own work using the four steps of art criticism.
2 POINTS	The student shows emerging awareness that artists use different colors to create landscapes.	The student shows emerging awareness of colors in the artwork and in the environment.	The student's drawing shows some use of different colors.	The student attempts to evaluate his or her own work but shows an incomplete understanding of evaluation criteria.
1 POINT	The student cannot recognize that artists use different colors to create landscapes.	The student does not locate colors in the artwork or in the environment.	The student's drawing does not show a variety of colors.	The student makes no attempt to evaluate his or her own artwork.

Level K • Unit 3 • Lesson 2

	Art History and Culture	Aesthetic Perception	Creative Expression	Art Criticism
3 POINTS	The student recognizes that artists with different styles get inspiration for their artwork from everyday objects.	The student accurately locates colors in the environment and identifies objects that are recognizable by color.	The student's collage clearly demonstrates using color to help make objects recognizable.	The student thoughtfully and honestly evaluates his or her own work using the four steps of art criticism.
2 POINTS	The student is sometimes able to recognize that artists with different styles get inspiration for their artwork from everyday objects.	The student shows emerging awareness of colors in the environment and can sometimes identify objects that are recognizable by color.	The student's collage shows some use of color to help make objects recognizable.	The student attempts to evaluate his or her own work but shows an incomplete understanding of evaluation criteria.
1 POINT	The student does not recognize that artists with different styles get inspiration for their artwork from everyday objects.	The student does not locate colors in the environment or identify objects that are recognizable by color.	The student's collage does not demonstrate using color to help make objects recognizable.	The student makes no attempt to evaluate his or her own artwork.

Level K   Creative Expression Rubrics

Name _____ Date _____ Lesson _____

Creative Expression Rubrics

Level K • Unit 3 • Lesson 3

	Art History and Culture	Aesthetic Perception	Creative Expression	Art Criticism
3 POINTS	The student recognizes that artists use many colors in their paintings.	The student identifies colors in fine art and in the environment.	The student's collage clearly demonstrates his or her recognition of the assigned color.	The student thoughtfully and honestly evaluates his or her own work using the four steps of art criticism.
2 POINTS	The student shows emerging awareness that artists use many colors in their paintings.	With teacher help the student identifies colors in fine art and in the environment.	The student's collage shows some recognition of the assigned color.	The student attempts to evaluate his or her own work but shows an incomplete understanding of evaluation criteria.
1 POINT	The student does not recognize that artists use many colors in their paintings.	The student does not identify colors in fine art or in the environment.	The student's collage does not demonstrate recognition of the assigned color.	The student makes no attempt to evaluate his or her own artwork.

Level K • Unit 3 • Lesson 4

	Art History and Culture	Aesthetic Perception	Creative Expression	Art Criticism
3 POINTS	The student compares how different artists use primary colors in their art.	The student identifies how the primary colors are used in various types of art.	The student's drawing clearly demonstrates primary colors.	The student thoughtfully and honestly evaluates his or her own work using the four steps of art criticism.
2 POINTS	The student shows emerging awareness of how different artists use primary colors in their art.	The student shows emerging awareness of how the primary colors are used in various types of art.	The student's drawing shows some use of primary colors.	The student attempts to evaluate his or her own work but shows an incomplete understanding of evaluation criteria.
1 POINT	The student cannot compare how different artists use primary colors in their art.	The student does not identify how the primary colors are used in various types of art.	The student's drawing does not demonstrate primary colors.	The student makes no attempt to evaluate his or her own artwork.

Name _____ Date _____ Lesson _____

Creative Expression Rubrics

Level K • Unit 3 • Lesson 5

	Art History and Culture	Aesthetic Perception	Creative Expression	Art Criticism
3 POINTS	The student recognizes that artists use bright and dull colors to express feelings in their works of art.	The student recognizes that artists use colors to express feelings.	The student's artwork clearly demonstrates the use of color to show a feeling.	The student thoughtfully and honestly evaluates his or her own work using the four steps of art criticism.
2 POINTS	The student shows emerging awareness that artists use bright and dull colors to express feelings in their works of art.	The student shows emerging awareness that artists use colors to express feelings.	The student's artwork shows some use of color to show a feeling.	The student attempts to evaluate his or her own work but shows an incomplete understanding of evaluation criteria.
1 POINT	The student cannot recognize that artists use bright and dull colors to express feelings in their works of art.	The student does not recognize that artists use colors to express feelings.	The student artwork does not demonstrate the use of color to show a feeling.	The student makes no attempt to evaluate his or her own artwork.

Level K • Unit 3 • Lesson 6

	Art History and Culture	Aesthetic Perception	Creative Expression	Art Criticism
3 POINTS	The student recognizes that artists have different styles for depicting water in art.	The student accurately locates light and dark values in the fine art.	The student's painting clearly demonstrates light and dark values.	The student thoughtfully and honestly evaluates his or her own work using the four steps of art criticism.
2 POINTS	The student shows emerging awareness that artists have different styles for depicting water in art.	The student shows emerging awareness of light and dark values and can identify some in the fine art.	The student's painting shows some use of light and dark values.	The student attempts to evaluate his or her own work but shows an incomplete understanding of evaluation criteria.
1 POINT	The student does not recognize that artists have different styles for depicting water in art.	The student does not locate light and dark values in the fine art.	The student's painting does not demonstrate light and dark values.	The student makes no attempt to evaluate his or her own artwork.

Name _____ Date _____ Lesson _____

Creative Expression Rubrics

Level K • Unit 4 • Lesson 1

	Art History and Culture	Aesthetic Perception	Creative Expression	Art Criticism
3 POINTS	The student recognizes a few facts about the art and life of Raoul Dufy and Edward Hopper.	The student accurately locates spaces in the artwork and in the environment.	The student's drawing clearly illustrates space.	The student thoughtfully and honestly evaluates his or her own work using the four steps of art criticism.
2 POINTS	The student shows emerging awareness of facts about the art and life of Raoul Dufy and Edward Hopper.	The student shows emerging ability to locate spaces in the artwork and in the environment.	The student's drawing shows some awareness of space.	The student attempts to evaluate his or her own work but shows an incomplete understanding of evaluation criteria.
1 POINT	The student does not recognize facts about the art and life of Raoul Dufy and Edward Hopper.	The student cannot locate spaces in the artwork or in the environment.	The student's drawing shows no understanding of space.	The student makes no attempt to evaluate his or her own artwork.

Level K • Unit 4 • Lesson 2

	Art History and Culture	Aesthetic Perception	Creative Expression	Art Criticism
3 POINTS	The student recognizes a few facts about the art and life of Felipa Trujillo.	The student accurately locates forms in the environment.	The student's clay form demonstrates a strong understanding of form.	The student thoughtfully and honestly evaluates his or her own work using the four steps of art criticism.
2 POINTS	The student shows emerging awareness of facts about the art and life of Felipa Trujillo.	The student shows emerging ability to locate forms in the environment.	The student's clay form demonstrates emerging awareness of form.	The student attempts to evaluate his or her own work but shows an incomplete understanding of evaluation criteria.
1 POINT	The student does not recognize facts about the art and life of Felipa Trujillo.	The student does not locate forms in the environment.	The student's clay form demonstrates no understanding of form.	The student makes no attempt to evaluate his or her own artwork.

Name _____ Date _____ Lesson _____

Creative Expression Rubrics

Level K • Unit 4 • Lesson 3

	Art History and Culture	Aesthetic Perception	Creative Expression	Art Criticism
3 POINTS	The student recognizes that artists have different styles for creating sculpture and can identify some of these differences in the fine art.	The student recognizes that sculptures are forms.	The student's puppet demonstrates a strong understanding of space and form.	The student thoughtfully and honestly evaluates his or her own work using the four steps of art criticism.
2 POINTS	The student shows emerging awareness of artists using different styles to create sculpture and can identify some of these differences in the fine art with help.	The student shows emerging ability to recognize that sculptures are forms.	The student's puppet demonstrates emerging awareness of space and form.	The student attempts to evaluate his or her own work but shows an incomplete understanding of evaluation criteria.
1 POINT	The student does not recognize that artists have different styles for creating sculpture and cannot identify these differences in the fine art.	The student does not recognize that sculptures are forms.	The student's puppet demonstrates no understanding of space and form.	The student makes no attempt to evaluate his or her own artwork.

Level K • Unit 4 • Lesson 4

	Art History and Culture	Aesthetic Perception	Creative Expression	Art Criticism
3 POINTS	The student recognizes that architecture is the art of designing and creating buildings.	The student accurately locates and identifies building forms in their environment.	The student's house sculpture demonstrates a strong understanding of building form.	The student thoughtfully and honestly evaluates his or her own work using the four steps of art criticism.
2 POINTS	The student shows emerging awareness of architecture being the art of designing and creating buildings.	The student shows emerging ability to locate and identify building forms in their environment.	The student's house sculpture demonstrates emerging awareness of building form.	The student attempts to evaluate his or her own work but shows an incomplete understanding of evaluation criteria.
1 POINT	The student does not recognize that architecture is the art of designing and creating buildings.	The student does not locate or identify building forms in their environment.	The student's house sculpture demonstrates no understanding of building form.	The student makes no attempt to evaluate his or her own artwork.

Name _____ Date _____ Lesson _____

Creative Expression Rubrics

Level K • Unit 4 • Lesson 5

	Art History and Culture	Aesthetic Perception	Creative Expression	Art Criticism
3 POINTS	The student recognizes that *William* is a sculpture from ancient Egypt.	The student accurately identifies four-legged animals that could be used as the subjects of a sculpture.	The student's animal sculpture demonstrates a strong understanding of form.	The student thoughtfully and honestly evaluates his or her own work using the four steps of art criticism.
2 POINTS	The student shows emerging awareness that *William* is a sculpture from ancient Egypt.	The student shows emerging ability to identify four-legged animals that could be used as the subjects of a sculpture.	The student's animal sculpture demonstrates emerging awareness of form.	The student attempts to evaluate his or her own work but shows an incomplete understanding of evaluation criteria.
1 POINT	The student does not recognize that *William* is a sculpture from ancient Egypt.	The student does not identify four-legged animals that could be used as the subjects of a sculpture.	The student's animal sculpture demonstrates no understanding of form.	The student makes no attempt to evaluate his or her own artwork.

Level K • Unit 4 • Lesson 6

	Art History and Culture	Aesthetic Perception	Creative Expression	Art Criticism
3 POINTS	The student recognizes that some art forms have a practical, useful purpose.	The student identifies artwork that has everyday uses.	The student's pinch pot is a sculpture that can be used.	The student thoughtfully and honestly evaluates his or her own work using the four steps of art criticism.
2 POINTS	The student shows emerging awareness that some art forms have a practical, useful purpose.	The student shows emerging ability to identify artwork that has everyday uses.	The student's pinch pot demonstrates emerging awareness of sculptures that can be used.	The student attempts to evaluate his or her own work but shows an incomplete understanding of evaluation criteria.
1 POINT	The student does not recognize that some art forms have a practical, useful purpose.	The student does not identify artwork that has everyday uses.	The student's pinch pot is not a sculpture that can be used.	The student makes no attempt to evaluate his or her own artwork.

Name _____ Date _____ Lesson _____

Creative Expression Rubrics

Level K • Unit 5 • Lesson 1

	Art History and Culture	Aesthetic Perception	Creative Expression	Art Criticism
3 POINTS	The student recognizes that artists use a variety of materials to create texture.	The student locates and verbally describes textures in the environment.	The student's collage clearly illustrates the use of textured materials.	The student thoughtfully and honestly evaluates his or her own work using the four steps of art criticism.
2 POINTS	The student show emerging awareness that artists use a variety of materials to create texture.	The student can sometimes locate and verbally describe textures in the environment.	The student's collage shows some use of textured materials.	The student attempts to evaluate his or her own work but shows an incomplete understanding of evaluation criteria.
1 POINT	The student does not recognize that artists use a variety of materials to create texture.	The student cannot locate or verbally describe texture in the environment.	The student's collage shows no use of textured materials.	The student makes no attempt to evaluate his or her own artwork.

Level K • Unit 5 • Lesson 2

	Art History and Culture	Aesthetic Perception	Creative Expression	Art Criticism
3 POINTS	The student accurately compares the use of visual texture in historical portraits.	The student accurately identifies and describes visual texture in fine art.	The student's crayon rubbing clearly shows visual texture.	The student thoughtfully and honestly evaluates his or her own work using the four steps of art criticism.
2 POINTS	The student shows emerging awareness of the use of visual texture in historical portraits.	The student shows emerging awareness of visual texture in fine art.	The student's crayon rubbing shows emerging awareness of visual texture.	The student attempts to evaluate his or her own work but shows an incomplete understanding of evaluation criteria.
1 POINT	The student cannot accurately compare the use of visual texture in historical portraits.	The student cannot accurately identify or describe visual texture.	The student's crayon rubbing does not show visual texture.	The student makes no attempt to evaluate his or her own artwork.

Level K — Creative Expression Rubrics

Name _____ Date _____ Lesson _____

Creative Expression Rubrics

Level K • Unit 5 • Lesson 3

	Art History and Culture	Aesthetic Perception	Creative Expression	Art Criticism
3 POINTS	The student recognizes that artists throughout history have used different textures to create puppets and toys.	The student accurately locates and describes texture in the environment.	The student's puppet clearly shows the use of different textures.	The student thoughtfully and honestly evaluates his or her own work using the four steps of art criticism.
2 POINTS	The student shows emerging awareness that artists throughout history have used different textures to create puppets and toys.	The student shows emerging awareness of texture in the environment.	The student's puppet shows some use of different textures.	The student attempts to evaluate his or her own work but shows an incomplete understanding of evaluation criteria.
1 POINT	The student shows no understanding that artists throughout history have used different textures to create puppets and toys.	The student cannot locate or describe texture in the environment.	The student's puppet does not show the use of different textures.	The student makes no attempt to evaluate his or her own artwork.

Level K • Unit 5 • Lesson 4

	Art History and Culture	Aesthetic Perception	Creative Expression	Art Criticism
3 POINTS	The student recognizes that baskets are made by people around the world.	The student accurately identifies fiber textures in art and the environment.	The student's basket clearly shows woven texture.	The student thoughtfully and honestly evaluates his or her own work using the four steps of art criticism.
2 POINTS	The student shows emerging awareness that baskets are made by people around the world.	The student shows emerging awareness of fiber textures in art and the environment.	The student's basket shows some texture but the weaving is incomplete.	The student attempts to evaluate his or her own work but shows an incomplete understanding of evaluation criteria.
1 POINT	The student does not recognize that baskets are made by people around the world.	The student cannot identify fiber textures in art or the environment.	The student's basket does not show woven texture.	The student makes no attempt to evaluate his or her own artwork.

Name _____ Date _____ Lesson _____

Creative Expression Rubrics

Level K • Unit 5 • Lesson 5

	Art History and Culture	Aesthetic Perception	Creative Expression	Art Criticism
3 POINTS	The student recognizes that artists from different cultures add real texture to forms.	The student accurately identifies and describes texture on three-dimensional objects.	The student's form clearly shows the use of real texture.	The student thoughtfully and honestly evaluates his or her own work using the four steps of art criticism.
2 POINTS	The student shows emerging awareness that artists from different cultures add real texture to forms.	The student shows emerging awareness of texture on three-dimensional objects.	The student's form shows some use of real texture.	The student attempts to evaluate his or her own work but shows an incomplete understanding of evaluation criteria.
1 POINT	The student shows no awareness that artists from different cultures add real texture to forms.	The student cannot identify or describe texture on three-dimensional objects.	The student's form does not show the use of texture.	The student makes no attempt to evaluate his or her own artwork.

Level K • Unit 5 • Lesson 6

	Art History and Culture	Aesthetic Perception	Creative Expression	Art Criticism
3 POINTS	The student demonstrates understanding that quilting and needlework are art forms.	The student can recognize textured stitchery in his or her environment.	The student's work clearly shows stitched texture.	The student thoughtfully and honestly evaluates his or her own work using the four steps of art criticism.
2 POINTS	The student shows emerging awareness that quilting and needlework are art forms.	The student shows emerging awareness of textured stitchery in his or her environment.	The student's work shows some stitched texture.	The student attempts to evaluate his or her own work but shows an incomplete understanding of evaluation criteria.
1 POINT	The student shows no awareness that quilting and needlework are art forms.	The student cannot recognize textured stitchery in his or her environment.	The student's work shows no stitched texture.	The student makes no attempt to evaluate his or her own artwork.

Level K   Creative Expression Rubrics

Name _____ Date _____ Lesson _____

Creative Expression Rubrics

Level K • Unit 6 • Lesson 1

	Art History and Culture	Aesthetic Perception	Creative Expression	Art Criticism
3 POINTS	The student recognizes that architects are artists who draw designs for homes and other buildings.	The student locates patterns in fine art and in his or her environment.	The student's drawing clearly illustrates use of patterns.	The student thoughtfully and honestly evaluates his or her own work using the four steps of art criticism.
2 POINTS	The student shows emerging awareness that architects are artists who draw designs for homes and other buildings.	The student can sometimes locate patterns in fine art and in his or her environment.	The student's drawing shows some use of patterns.	The student attempts to evaluate his or her own work but shows an incomplete understanding of evaluation criteria.
1 POINT	The student does not recognize that architects are artists who draw designs for homes and other buildings.	The student cannot locate patterns in fine art or in his or her environment.	The student's drawing shows no use of patterns.	The student makes no attempt to evaluate his or her own artwork.

Level K • Unit 6 • Lesson 2

	Art History and Culture	Aesthetic Perception	Creative Expression	Art Criticism
3 POINTS	The student identifies how Savitsky and Currier and Ives showed rhythm and movement in the fine art in this lesson.	The student can explain how rhythm creates the look of movement.	The student's drawing clearly illustrates rhythm and movement.	The student thoughtfully and honestly evaluates his or her own work using the four steps of art criticism.
2 POINTS	The student shows emerging awareness of how Savitsky and Currier and Ives showed rhythm and movement in the fine art in this lesson.	The student can give some explanation of how rhythm creates the look of movement.	The student's drawing shows some rhythm and movement.	The student attempts to evaluate his or her own work but shows an incomplete understanding of evaluation criteria.
1 POINT	The student cannot identify how Savitsky or Currier and Ives showed rhythm and movement in the fine art in this lesson.	The student cannot explain how rhythm creates the look of movement.	The student's drawing shows no rhythm or movement.	The student makes no attempt to evaluate his or her own artwork.

Name _____ Date _____ Lesson _____

Creative Expression Rubrics

Level K • Unit 6 • Lesson 3

	Art History and Culture	Aesthetic Perception	Creative Expression	Art Criticism
3 POINTS	The student recognizes that artists from different cultures use even balance in their designs.	The student can locate even balance in an object and verbally describe how the object is balanced.	The student's design clearly illustrates even balance.	The student thoughtfully and honestly evaluates his or her own work using the four steps of art criticism.
2 POINTS	The student shows emerging awareness that artists from different cultures use even balance in their designs.	The student can sometimes locate even balance in an object and verbally describe how the object is balanced.	The student's design shows some balance.	The student attempts to evaluate his or her own work but shows an incomplete understanding of evaluation criteria.
1 POINT	The student does not recognize that artists from different cultures use even balance in their designs.	The student cannot locate even balance in an object or verbally describe how the object is balanced.	The student's design shows no balance.	The student makes no attempt to evaluate his or her own artwork.

Level K • Unit 6 • Lesson 4

	Art History and Culture	Aesthetic Perception	Creative Expression	Art Criticism
3 POINTS	The student recognizes how artists from different cultures use balance in their sculptures.	The student can recognize sculptures that have balance.	The student's house post clearly illustrates balance.	The student thoughtfully and honestly evaluates his or her own work using the four steps of art criticism.
2 POINTS	The student shows emerging awareness of how artists from different cultures use balance in their sculptures.	The student can sometimes recognize sculptures that have balance.	The student's house post shows some balance.	The student attempts to evaluate his or her own work but shows an incomplete understanding of evaluation criteria.
1 POINT	The student cannot recognize how artists from different cultures use balance in their sculptures.	The student cannot recognize sculptures that have balance.	The student's house post shows no balance.	The student makes no attempt to evaluate his or her own artwork.

Level K   Creative Expression Rubrics

Name _____ Date _____ Lesson _____

Creative Expression Rubrics

Level K • Unit 6 • Lesson 5

	Art History and Culture	Aesthetic Perception	Creative Expression	Art Criticism
3 POINTS	The student recognizes that artists from similar cultures have different styles of painting.	The student can recognize unity in fine art and verbally describe why the artwork has unity.	The student's composition clearly illustrates unity.	The student thoughtfully and honestly evaluates his or her own work using the four steps of art criticism.
2 POINTS	The student shows emerging awareness that artists from similar cultures have different styles of painting.	The student can sometimes recognize unity in fine art and verbally describe why the artwork has unity.	The student's composition shows emerging awareness of unity.	The student attempts to evaluate his or her own work but shows an incomplete understanding of evaluation criteria.
1 POINT	The student cannot recognize that artists from similar cultures have different styles of painting.	The student cannot recognize unity in fine art or verbally describe why the artwork has unity.	The student's composition shows no unity.	The student makes no attempt to evaluate his or her own artwork.

Level K • Unit 6 • Lesson 6

	Art History and Culture	Aesthetic Perception	Creative Expression	Art Criticism
3 POINTS	The student recognizes that artists from different cultures show different activities in their art.	The student can recognize unity in sculpture and verbally describe why a sculpture has unity.	The student's sculpture clearly illustrates unity and is an effective part of a unified installation.	The student thoughtfully and honestly evaluates his or her own work using the four steps of art criticism.
2 POINTS	The student shows emerging awareness that artists from different cultures show different activities in their art.	The student can sometimes recognize unity in sculpture and verbally describe why a sculpture has unity.	The student's sculpture shows emerging awareness of unity and is somewhat effective as part of a unified installation.	The student attempts to evaluate his or her own work but shows an incomplete understanding of evaluation criteria.
1 POINT	The student does not recognize that artists from different cultures show different activities in their art.	The student cannot recognize unity in sculpture or verbally describe why a sculpture has unity.	The student's sculpture shows no unity and is not an effective part of a unified installation.	The student makes no attempt to evaluate his or her own artwork.